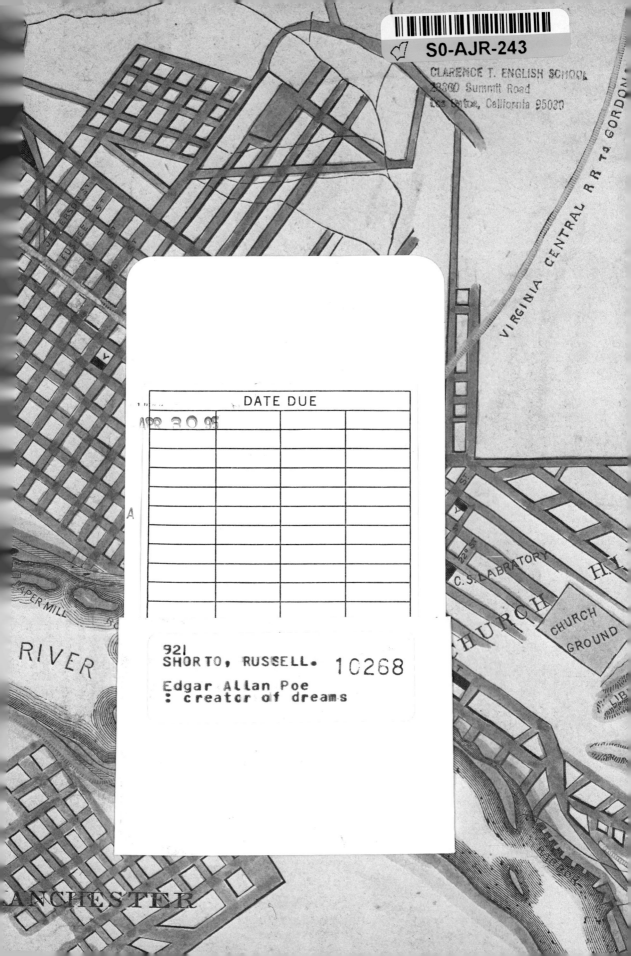

VIRGINIA CENTRAL RR to GORDON

DATE DUE

APR 30 95			

RIVER

ANCHESTER

"Thank Heaven! the crisis—
The danger is past,
And the lingering illness
Is over at last—
And the fever called 'Living'
Is conquered at last."

CLASSIC AUTHORS SERIES

EDGAR ALLAN POE
Creator of Dreams

———•———

By Russell Shorto
FOREWORD BY LEO LEMAY, PH.D.

THE KIPLING PRESS · NEW YORK

This book is dedicated to
Mr. William Stahl
former English teacher,
Westmont Hilltop Junior High School
Johnstown, Pennsylvania.

Copyright © 1988 by Russell Shorto
Cover illustration copyright © 1988 by Mark Summers
Illustrations copyright © 1988 by Mark Corcoran
Photo credits: Pp. ii, viii, 8, 16, 21, 39 courtesy of the University
of Virginia Library; pp. 23, 46 courtesy of the Bronx County
Historical Society, NYC; p. 32 courtesy of Culver Pictures; p. 37
courtesy of Historical Pictures Service, Chicago.
The endpaper map is a detail of Richmond, Virginia
in the 19th century.

Printed in the United States
ISBN 0-943718-10-4

The Kipling Press
First Edition

FOREWORD

dgar Allan Poe wrote the scariest stories in the English language. The reason that they are so memorable and frightening is that they reverberate in the reader's mind and imagination.

A few critics in Poe's own time thought his stories, like "The Cask of Amontillado," "The Pit and the Pendulum," and "The Fall of the House of Usher," so strange and different that they supposed Poe must be imitating the style and mood of some German authors. When Poe heard about the supposed German influence, he replied, "Terror is not of Germany but of the soul." Evidently Poe himself thought that what he was doing in these stories was reaching the very sources of fear present in every person's soul.

Besides being a master of horror, Edgar Allan Poe created the detective story. C. Augustus Dupin, the main character in "The Murders in the Rue Morgue," "The Purloined Letter," and "The Mystery of Marie Roget," supplied Sir Arthur Conan Doyle with the model for his great character Sherlock Holmes. "The Gold Bug," a tale of buried treasure and of a map written in code, is another of Poe's best-known detective stories.

Although Poe is most famous in the twentieth century for his stories, he thought of himself primarily as a poet. His melodramatic "The Raven" was the most popular American poem of the nineteenth century. Poe's excellent and distinctive, though somewhat small, body of poetry makes him one of the dominant poets of nineteenth-century American literature. His poetry set the stage for the entirely different kinds of poetry written by Walt Whitman and Emily Dickinson. The great Irish poet of the next generation, William Butler Yeats, said that Poe was "always and for all lands a great lyric poet."

He was also the greatest American literary critic of the nineteenth century. Because of the savagery of his criticism, he was known as "The Tomahawk Man." He would ridicule the efforts of the bad writers of his time, pointing out specific misuses of words. He would also, at times, rewrite lines of the poetry he was reviewing, showing how they could and should have been better done. He would criticize the plots of novels, pointing out their weaknesses. But when he encountered a great writer like Charles Dickens, whose work was little known at the time, Poe recognized his genius and gave him great praise.

Poe was also America's first important theoretical critic. He defined what a short story should be and then analyzed Nathaniel Hawthorne's stories in accordance with his definition. In "The Philosophy of Composition," "The Rationale of Verse," and "The Poetic Principle," he set forth his own theories of literature, condemning moralistic literature, arguing for art for art's sake, and maintaining that the greatest artist could completely control the mind and emotions of the reader.

Although Edgar Allan Poe died at the early age of forty, he left behind a major body of writings. It is one of the ironies of his career that during his lifetime, he was more widely celebrated as a major writer in England and especially in France than he was in America, his homeland.

— *J.A. Leo Lamay*
University of Delaware
April 4, 1988

Engraving of Poe by John Sartain of Philadelphia

ONCE UPON A MIDNIGHT

"Her life was despaired of. I took leave of her forever,
and underwent all the agonies of her death."

Black shadows hung thick in all the corners of the room. The only light in the room was from the massive flickering fireplace. Outside, a howling wind whipped around the house, sounding like the whispered cries of bats or demons trying to get in. The heavy purple drapes over the windows were like a wall that kept them out.

A thin, pale man dressed all in black sat slumped in an overstuffed chair staring into the fire. His gaze was so intense that one might have thought he was a doll or man-

1

nequin propped up in a chair. At last, however, he blinked, and as he did tears of sadness squeezed out of his eyes and rolled down the gaunt, slack cheeks.

His name was Edgar Poe. He was a young writer who had recently won some fame for a collection of stories. A proud and often arrogant man, Poe firmly believed that he was the greatest writer America had yet produced. After years of struggle, others were finally taking notice of him. But aside from recognition, he had earned almost nothing from his writing. His book, *Tales of the Grotesque and Arabesque*, became one of the most popular short story collections ever published. He was paid only in copies of the book. He received no money at all.

He wouldn't have minded this situation as much if he had only himself to support. But his wife and her mother depended on him. The two women worshipped him and sat for hours listening as he read his latest poem or story to them. Poe loved his family and was happy to care for them. He had gotten a job as an editor and for a time all had gone well. Then his drinking had gotten him into trouble again and he'd been fired.

It was not money or fame that concerned him now. In the next room his beautiful wife lay dying. The thought of his precious, fragile Virginia wracked with the dreaded tuberculosis tore at his heart and mind. It drove him nearly mad. Virginia was his one link to the real world, the world in which people woke in the morning, talked, ate, worked, and did a thousand other ordinary things. Poe knew that his mind was unstable, filled with weird and twisted visions of life and death that threatened to spill out and engulf him. Without Virginia's calm influence, he feared the visions would take control and drive him insane.

Sitting in his chair, Poe's mind swirled with thoughts of the pain his sweet wife was going through and of her death that was sure to come. Suddenly he was startled by a sharp CLACK!

CLACK! outside the window. He leaned back when he realized it was only the wind blowing the shutter against the window. Then he stiffened again as new thoughts raced through his teeming brain. Jumping to his feet, he ran to his desk and picked up a pen. The pen bled its ink across the paper. Poe, breathing feverishly, smiled through his clenched teeth as he watched the words pour out.

> Once upon a midnight dreary,
>   while I pondered, weak and weary
> Over many a quaint and curious volume
>   of forgotten lore—
> While I nodded, nearly napping
>   suddenly there came a tapping,
> As of some one gently rapping, rapping at my chamber door.

It was the beginning of a great, eerie, droning poem of death and sadness. It would be called "The Raven" and it would make Poe once and for all a master among American writers. In the poem, a man expresses his torment over the death of his love, his "sorrow for the lost Lenore."

Although Poe's own wife Virginia was not yet dead, he was already nearly smothered with the pain of losing her. He knew well the feeling of losing a woman so close to him because this was not the first time it had happened. Long ago, when Edgar was a rollicking infant, the same horrible scene had played itself out. Then, a young woman about the age of Virginia had died of the same disease. The sudden loss of his mother had confused and terrified the young Edgar. It had marked forever his life and his writing.

lizabeth Poe, Edgar's mother, had been an actress and her husband, David, an actor. For several years after 1800, the two worked together in a company that traveled through the cities up and down the east coast of the young United States of America. David was a fair actor who played minor characters in the company's plays. When he wasn't on stage, he was usually in pubs near the theaters, drinking with whomever happened to be at hand.

Elizabeth, however, was a brilliant young actress who played the leading female role in all the company's plays. When they performed *Romeo and Juliet*, she was Juliet. Newspapers in every city gave the delicate, winsome Elizabeth Poe rave reviews for her stunning performances. She was the company's main attraction.

Nevertheless, the couple was desperately poor and, in 1807, when Elizabeth gave birth to a son, William, their situation became even more difficult. Two years later, in 1809, while the company was in Boston performing Shakespeare's *Hamlet*, Elizabeth bore her second son, whom she named Edgar. The little family was so poor that Elizabeth had to perform right up until the night the baby was born.

Soon after Edgar's birth, David Poe, whose drinking problem

had grown worse, left his young wife and family, never to return. Later that year Elizabeth gave birth to a daughter, Rosalie. The poor woman was now left by herself to care for three infant children while working as an actress nearly every evening. What was more, the pregnancies had weakened her frail body. Unable to manage three children, she left William with his grandparents.

Edgar, now nearly three years old, was completely unaware of the tremendous hardship his mother faced. For the young boy, life was thrilling. There were new places to explore every week; there was the excitement of seeing his mother dressed up in fancy costumes. To him, the most beautiful woman in the world was his lovely, devoted mother. His whole world was centered around her.

Then, suddenly, she was gone. She died of tuberculosis, the most fearful disease of the day. It killed its victim by attacking the lungs and slowly weakening the body. For many days Elizabeth had lain in bed, her face flushed with fever and her eyes shining with an unearthly brilliance. Then, to Edgar's terror, she vanished.

This image of a feverish, beautiful, dying woman was to haunt Edgar Poe all his life, for it was the last one he would have of his mother.

A DEMON IN MY MIND

"From childhood's hour I have not been
As others were—I have not seen
As others saw—I could not bring
My passions from a common spring—"

Elizabeth Poe died in Richmond, Virginia. At that time a woman named Frances Allan lived in Richmond. Frances Allan was unable to have children of her own. The moment she saw the pretty young son of Elizabeth Poe she fell in love with him and determined to adopt him. So it was that Edgar, at age three, suddenly found himself with a new mother. He was taken into the Allan household and showered with love. Soon the image of his real mother blurred and mingled with that of Frances Allan, whom he called "Ma."

But John Allan, Frances' husband, was a different story. He was a dour, stony-faced businessman who had little love for children. He accepted Edgar into his house only because his wife insisted upon it. But he made up his own mind that, while the boy could live in the house, he would never become a member of his family. Edgar Poe, this actor's brat, was no son of his. John Allan, though he was now the boy's protector, would always bring Edgar pain and hardship. He was like a cloud that Poe later wrote about which took the form of "a demon in my view."

The Allans were a wealthy family, and Edgar grew up among the polite society of Richmond. He rode a fine horse and had his own pack of dogs that he loved to run. He had inherited some of his parents' love of acting. When the Allans had guests he would delight the adults by standing on the dining table, dressed in finery, and reciting little speeches. When he finished, everyone would clap loudly and Edgar would bow solemnly, his ears burning with pleasure.

John Allan's company, Ellis & Allan, made its money in shipping goods. A large part of his firm's business was in shipping tobacco to England. During the War of 1812, all shipments from America to Europe were cut off, which hurt Allan's business. By 1815, however, trade had resumed, and John Allan decided to take a voyage to England to inspect the markets there for himself. With him went his wife and six-year-old Edgar.

Edgar's next five years were spent in England. He did not live with the Allans. He stayed at an old school called Manor House at Stoke Newington, just outside London. Only occasionally was he allowed to visit Mrs. Allan, whom he now loved almost as much as he had loved his mother. For five important childhood years Edgar lived without the love and warmth of a family. In its place was the school.

Those five years in England made an enormous impression on Poe as a writer. The stories he later wrote are very different from those of other American writers of the time. In fact, to many people Poe does not seem like an American writer at all. His writing was greatly influenced by the history and legends of old England, and by the country's buildings.

Poe wrote about the school and the town in a story called "William Wilson."

Poe in his school years

> My earliest recollec-
> tions of a school life,
> are connected with a
> large, rambling, Eliza-
> bethan house, in a
> misty-looking village
> of England, where
> were a vast number of gigantic and gnarled trees, and where
> all the houses were excessively ancient.

The main building of the school dated from the days of Shakespeare, more than two hundred years before Edgar's birth. The schoolroom was long and narrow. Its high-peaked Gothic windows looked out on a sky that seemed forever cloudy. The students' bedrooms were in the same building. After class, Edgar would tramp through the narrow halls, up dimly-lit staircases, and through a maze of passages before reaching his tiny room.

Young Edgar did not find this dark and misty place depressing. It seemed to suit him. He wrote:

In truth, it was a dream-like and spirit-soothing place, that venerable old town. At this moment, in fancy, I feel the refreshing chillness of its deeply-shadowed avenues, inhale the fragrance of its thousand shrubberies, and thrill anew with undefinable delight, at the deep hollow note of the church-bell breaking each hour, with sullen and sudden roar, upon the stillness of the dusky atmosphere in which the fretted Gothic steeple lay embedded and asleep.

In this place Edgar studied Latin and French, and his young spirit grew in the atmosphere of ancient things and times.

In 1820, John Allan suddenly decided that his business in England was finished. That same year the family returned to Richmond. Back in America, Edgar spent more of his time with

the Allans. But all was not well. Mrs. Allan had fallen ill, and it was feared that she had fallen prey to tuberculosis.

John Allan, meanwhile, now had the opportunity to study young Edgar and see what kind of youth the boy had turned into. He was not pleased. Edgar had developed a taste for playing pranks and for bragging. John Allan tried to beat these bad habits out of the boy, but he only succeeded in increasing Edgar's opposition to him.

Also, the boy had somehow developed a passion for, of all things, poetry. To the hard-minded, practical John Allan, there was no more foolish waste of time than writing poetry. Further, Edgar's dreamy, sensitive nature grated on the man. A boy, he believed, should be tough-skinned in order to prepare himself for the business world. Edgar's fascination with poetry, death, sadness, and love seemed unnatural and unhealthy to the practical businessman.

Still, Edgar wrote. As Frances Allan grew sicker, the tension between her husband and her beloved Edgar grew stronger. Finally, they could stand one another no more. When Edgar was seventeen years old, John Allan decided to get the boy out of his sight by enrolling him as a student at the University of Virginia.

Edgar was overjoyed at the thought of attending university and living the life of a scholar. It would be a new world of experiences, and, equally important, it would free him from the beatings and the incessant glare of his foster father.

EDGAR ALLAN PERRY, LE RENNET, POE, A BOSTONIAN

"Send me I entreat you some money immediately, as I am in the greatest necessity. If you fail to comply with my request—I tremble for the consequence."

In 1826, the University of Virginia was not the oldest or the most prestigious university in the country at that time, but it was the most magnificent. It was designed by none other than Thomas Jefferson. Jefferson, besides having been a great statesman and the writer of the Declaration of Independence, was also a brilliant architect. He designed the buildings along the lines of the great classical structures of Greece and Rome. When it was finished, he called his noble creation "the Oxford of the New World."

When he came to Jefferson's university, Edgar Poe dove into his studies and the life of the student with great enthusiasm. A passionate lover of languages, he took classes in Latin, Greek, French, Spanish, and Italian, and he did well in all of them. However, attending the university was not merely a matter of studying and getting good grades. Only sons of wealthy gentlemen were able to afford the costs of a university education. Besides tuition, there were expenses for room and meals, as well as a servant. Then there was tailoring, laundry, and dozens of other things that a wealthy young man had to have in order to remain respectable.

It seemed that John Allan played a cruel joke on Edgar. He sent him off with only $110, knowing full well that the costs of attending the university would be at least $350. When Edgar wrote to his foster father explaining the situation and asking for more money, Allan ignored him. Within a very short time Edgar's money had dwindled to nothing. His beloved foster mother was far too ill to be bothered with this problem. He would have to get money on his own.

It was a custom among the young dandies at the university to gather at pubs and gamble for entertainment. Edgar was a popular fixture at these events. He was already noted among the others as a writer and a witty talker. Now that he was in such desperate need of money, it occurred to him that he might be able to win it from some of these wealthy young men. He began playing cards as often as possible, betting high stakes—and losing.

Within a short time he was in debt to almost everyone he knew. Out of funds, he had to ask the tradesmen of the town—the tailor, laundress, and bootmaker—to accept credit. He promised that he would pay later, and hoped and prayed that John Allan would eventually send more money.

His foster father never sent a penny, despite the fact that he had just inherited a fortune from an old uncle. Panicked by his dilemma, Edgar began drinking with his friends to forget his mounting problems. He never drank much. The smallest amount of "peach and honey"—an alcoholic Southern punch—was enough to make him drunk. As one of his friends said, "One glass at a time was all that he could take; but this was sufficient to rouse his whole nervous nature into a state of strongest excitement, which found vent in a continuous flow of wild, fascinating talk that irresistibly enchanted every listener with sire-like power."

So began Edgar Poe's drinking. Like his real father, whom Edgar could not remember, he would become a slave to it.

At the end of Edgar's first year at the university, his teachers awarded him "highest honors" in French and Latin. He was a remarkable student, but his first year was his last. John Allan eventually came to visit. Seeing the terrible financial state the boy had gotten himself in, Allan promptly removed him from the school and brought him home. It apparently never occurred to the man that he himself was to blame for the boy's debts.

When Edgar returned to Richmond he sought out a girl named Elmira Royster. Before leaving for school they had fallen in love and secretly promised each other that they would one day marry. While he was away they wrote to each other often. Soon John Allan and Mr. Royster found out about the affair and intercepted the letters. Both Edgar and Elmira were puzzled at not hearing from the other. Finally, Elmira's father forced her to marry another young man who was more stable than the starry-eyed son of an actor. Edgar returned to Richmond to find Elmira, his first love, the wife of another man. He was shattered, heartbroken, and convinced that John Allan was somehow at the bottom of the terrible business.

No sooner did Edgar return home than arguments broke out between him and his foster father. Edgar realized that he could not live with the man and would have to find some way to support himself. When he told John Allan that he wanted to seek his own fortune, Allan laughed in Edgar's face. What could a miserable, ungrateful, irresponsible brat hope to get out of life on his own? How would he earn a living? With his scribbling? Allan's bear-like frame shook with laughter, while the slim, pale young man before him trembled with rage.

His eyes blazing, Edgar vowed that, in fact, he would make a living from his writing. He would show Allan who was the fool!

The very next morning he kissed Mrs. Allan goodbye, calmly told his foster father that he was the poorest excuse for a man Edgar had ever known, then left the house, never to return.

Edgar went to stay for a short while with a friend in Richmond. He sent John Allan a letter that same day:

> *Sir,*
>
> *After my treatment on yesterday and what passed between us this morning, I can hardly think you will be surprised at the contents of this letter. My determination is at length taken to leave your house and endeavor to find some place in this wide world where I will be treated—not as you have treated me.*

Edgar finished by asking Allan to send him enough money to live on for a month until he could find a job. "If you still have the least affection for me," Edgar implored. He could not believe that Allan actually hated him, and he felt sure that his foster father would do this much for him. But, unchanged, Allan sent nothing.

Edgar then decided to seek his fortune northward. He booked passage to Boston on a coal ship, leaving Richmond and his ogre foster father behind him.

For some reason, he didn't record his real name in the ship's record. Instead, he called himself Henri Le Rennet. It was as though he wished to create a new life and personality for himself, and it was not the last time he would use a false name. When he was younger he had been somewhat confused as to what name to go by, Edgar Allan or Edgar Poe. He had decided on Edgar A. Poe. After all his real name was Poe, and not for anything would he take the name of John Allan.

Edgar's life in Boston began on a hopeful note, with the publishing of his first book of poetry. It was called *Tamerlane and Other Poems*, and when it came out in 1827 he was just 18. Again he did not use his name on the book. Instead he signed it

The writer in his twenties

"by a Bostonian." This wasn't entirely a lie, since he had been born in Boston. Poe had befriended a printer named Calin Thomas, who was himself only 19 years old, and had convinced him to publish the volume.

These first poems are rarely read today, but they have the haunting, lyrical quality that would eventually become the hallmark of Poe's style. Nevertheless, the book did not receive a single review in the press. Edgar A. Poe had made his first big splash, but no one seemed to take notice.

There were only fifty copies of the book printed, and even these few did not sell out. So the young author, without a cent in his pocket, was forced to search the streets for scraps of food. Today, the few original copies of *Tamerlane* are the most valuable of all rare American books. One of them would probably fetch hundreds of thousands of dollars.

Disappointed and in desperate need of a job, Poe next decided to enlist in the army. This time he used the name Edgar A. Perry.

One might think that such a headstrong, sensitive, dreamy young man would not do well in the rigid, orderly life of the army, but Poe proved to be a model soldier. He was quickly promoted from Private to Sergeant-Major. He was stationed for a time on Sullivan's Island, a tiny island in the harbor of Charleston, South Carolina. Years later he would write a clever story called "The Gold Bug," about two men who discover buried pirates' treasure on this island.

Just as Poe's life seemed at last to be improving, he received bad news from Richmond. Frances Allan, who had always been like a mother to him, finally died from tuberculosis. With deep sadness, Poe journeyed to Richmond to pay his last respects. At the funeral, John Allan did not even try to disguise his hatred for Edgar.

In 1830, Poe entered West Point, the U.S. military academy for the training of young officers. When he learned of this, Allan was pleased at the thought that the boy might make something of himself. Allan even sent money to help with expenses, and for a time all seemed well. But Edgar Poe seemed to have something inside of him that couldn't stand for things to go smoothly. After six months at West Point, he decided that the life of unending discipline was not one for a poet. He abruptly stopped going to classes and was dismissed. Allan, of course, was furious and declared that the young man was a hopeless fool. He promptly stopped Edgar's expense money.

Poe had cut himself off from the security of the army and Allan. He had no home, no money, and, with Frances Allan dead, no one who cared for him. But he still had his dream, his glorious dream of one day becoming a great writer surrounded by admirers. Yes, he dreamed, one day Edgar Allan Poe, alias Edgar A. Perry, alias Henri Le Rennet, "a Bostonian," would become known and loved by millions.

Yes, Edgar still had his dreams. What's more, he had recently discovered that he was not quite alone in the world after all. He had a family that he had never known.

The Rare and Radiant Maiden

*"I cannot express in words the fervent devotion I feel
towards my dear little cousin—my own darling."*

In his army days Edgar had passed through Baltimore, and there he had discovered a house full of Poes.  Here, in a ramshackle little building, lived his father's sister, Maria Clemm, and several other relatives. Mrs. Clemm was a poor woman but when Edgar showed up on her doorstep one day, without a job or a home, her heart went out to him and she took him in. No one who lived in the house was able to earn a regular living. Mrs. Clemm supported everyone as

best she could by doing housework.

Poe began writing for various newspapers to earn his keep. Whatever money he received he handed over to Mrs. Clemm. One of the members of the family was Mrs. Clemm's ten-year-old daughter Virginia. The girl soon developed a strong attachment to "Cousin Eddy," who seemed so awfully intelligent and who took her on long walks and read his poems to her.

Shortly after he moved in, Poe published his second book of poems, called *Al Aaraaf, Tamerlane, and Minor Poems*. A year later, his third book, *Poems by Edgar A. Poe*, came out. Both books received reviews in various newspapers. Within a short time, Edgar A. Poe became a popular fellow in the drawing rooms of Baltimore. He basked in the sudden attention and set out to prove himself a witty and entertaining young man at parties.

Despite moderate success, the Poe household was still desperately poor. Edgar's writings brought in very little money. His brother William was bedridden, as was Mrs. Clemm's old mother. Poe realized that poetry would never bring in very much money, so he decided to try his hand at writing short stories. In these days, before television and radio, all the newspapers ran stories, which were popular entertainment.

He published a few stories but none made much money. Then, in 1833, his story "MS Found in a Bottle" won first prize in a contest given by the Baltimore *Sunday Visitor*. The prize money was fifty dollars! This large sum rescued the family from starvation. Things had become so bad that Mrs. Clemm had been collecting rags to sell.

The fifty dollars was not all the contest brought Edgar. He also earned the admiration of several influential men of the city. One of the contest judges said of Edgar's stories, "There was genius in everything." Edgar, who always believed strongly in himself, agreed. Things seemed to be looking up.

In 1834, Edgar learned that John Allan had been ill for several years and was near death. Edgar had not heard from his foster father for some time, but, after learning of his condition, decided to visit him. John Allan had taken a second wife after Frances's death. When Edgar showed up at the door, he was greeted by this stern woman who told the young man, whom she did not recognize, that Mr. Allan was too ill to have visitors.

Edgar forced his way past her and rushed into the bedroom. Surely, he thought, now that his foster father was near death his feelings toward him would soften. In spite of how he'd been treated by Allan, Edgar's desire to be loved moved him to visit the man who had been so mean.

There, in a wide bed, lay John Allan—pale, weak, and obviously near death. But when he saw Edgar at the door his eyes lit up with hatred, and strength seemed to return to him. He grabbed his cane and waved it furiously at the young man. Edgar stood horrified, realizing once and for all that his foster father hated him and would never change. His heart filled with pain, Edgar fled from the house. Allan died a month later. He left a large fortune behind, but not one cent did he leave to the boy who had grown up in his care.

Edgar's literary prospects improved after winning the *Sunday Visitor* contest. By 1835, he sold several more stories. In August of that year, a magazine in Richmond called the *Southern Literary Messenger* accepted his application for a job as editor, which would pay him sixty dollars a month. At first Edgar was overjoyed at this news, but then his heart sank as he realized it would mean separation from Mrs. Clemm and Virginia. Mrs. Clemm, whom he called "Muddy," had become like a mother to him. Since he had never really had a warm, loving family as a child he clung desperately to her love and kindness. As for Virginia, now 13, Edgar had to admit to himself that, though she was still a girl, he had fallen hopelessly in love with her.

Nevertheless, the job offer was too good to pass up. Edgar left the home he had grown to love and settled in Richmond once again. Shortly after Edgar left, his cousin, Neilson Poe, offered to provide for Mrs. Clemm and Virginia by taking them into his own home. Neilson had also declared that he would educate Virginia. This news drove Edgar into a fury of anger and jealousy. He was lonely in Richmond without "Muddy" and Virginia. He believed that if they moved in with Neilson he would lose them forever.

Immediately he dashed off a letter begging his aunt and cousin to come to Richmond and live with him. In

Watercolor of Virginia Clemm

the letter he professed his deep love for Virginia and asked her to marry him. The two women, who both loved and pitied Edgar, decided to join him. Edgar sent them money for moving expenses and, once they were settled, arranged for marriage papers to be drawn up. He had to lie about Virginia's age on the documents, claiming that she was twenty-one. The papers were accepted, and Edgar A. Poe and Virginia Clemm were married on May 16, 1836. Poe was twenty-seven years old and Virginia was not yet fourteen.

At that time, it was not against the law to marry one's cousin. It was also not unusual for women to marry at a young age. However, few women married as young as Virginia did. The love they felt for one another was not typical, but it was very strong. Virginia saw her husband as a man of towering intelligence and great artistic talent. He was also a gallant, old-fashioned sort of man who protected her from difficulty and loved to do little things for her. He was more like an older brother than a husband.

For Edgar, although Virginia was not yet a woman, she was his "rare and radiant maiden," as he later wrote in "The Raven." He was not just her husband, but her protector and guardian. She would always be half-woman and half-child to him. He called her "Sis," even after they were married.

With Mrs. Clemm and his dear Virginia living with him, Edgar dove happily into his work at the *Messenger*. Oddly enough, the offices of the magazine were right next to the store operated by the firm of Ellis & Allan, John Allan's old company. Each day, Edgar walked by its storefront and smelled the odors of spices and tobacco that wafted out from its door. He chuckled occasionally to think that old John Allan never wanted him near his business and now he was working right next door to it. Then he would remember that last hateful look Allan gave him and his smile would vanish.

Edgar Allan Poe

Edgar soon made a name for himself as a reviewer of other people's writing. America was a young country and had few great writers. Most reviewers treated even mediocre books kindly in their reviews, but Poe demanded perfection. He would not lower himself to say meaningless kind things about poor writing. The *Southern Literary Messenger*'s circulation shot up as more and more people wanted to read the intelligent and delightfully nasty reviews of Edgar A. Poe. James Russell Lowell, a very important writer of the day, declared that, "Mr. Poe is at once the most discriminating, philosophical, and fearless critic upon imaginative works who has written in America." But he added that Poe "seems sometimes to mistake his phial of prussic-acid for his inkstand."

Poe outdid himself reviewing a novel by an up-and-coming writer from New England named Theodore Fay. His words sliced into the book like a surgeon cutting into a patient, and he laid out its weaknesses for all to see. In fact, it *was* a poorly written book, but the New England writers, who had great power in American literary circles, were outraged. They decided this crude, ill-mannered Poe fellow loved only his own work.

They were wrong about Poe. He was not out to destroy all writers but himself. He simply took his work as a reviewer and critic seriously. He was the first American critic to give a balanced examination of each work, showing its good and bad points, rather than be content with saying a few nice things about it. He read each book several times and analyzed it in great detail. He picked out phrases that were nicely or poorly used or that suggested the writer was careless. He did not write only negative reviews. He found many works, often by unknown writers, to be surprisingly good, and he said so.

All this while, Poe's reputation was growing. People who were attracted to him by his reviews sought out his stories. To their surprise, they found a world of terror and strangeness. These were quite unlike any stories they had read before. Readers all over the nation were fascinated.

Money continued to be a problem, however. Edgar had spent $200 to buy furniture for a boarding-house that Mrs. Clemm would operate, but the purchase of the house fell through and the little family was left with no savings. Then Edgar had an idea. The most popular author of the day in England was Charles Dickens. Dickens made good money writing novels that were serialized in certain magazines that carried a new chapter in every issue. Poe decided that he, too, would write a long work for serialization.

The book that resulted is *The Narrative of Arthur Gordon Pym*. It is a fantasy and a horror tale of a shipwreck. Poe mixed the story with scientific facts, as well as made-up facts. He came up with an ingenious introduction claiming that he, Edgar A. Poe, had been told the story by a sailor who had actually been on the voyage. It was so convincing, many readers believed it was a true story.

Now Edgar, Virginia, and Mrs. Clemm were a happy little family. They lived together in a comfortable little house. In the evenings Mrs. Clemm cooked a nice dinner, and afterwards they all sat around the fire while Virginia played the harp and sang in her sweet, thin voice.

Poe had a happy home life for the first time ever, but he began drinking again. As an editor for an up-and-coming magazine—and as the man most responsible for the magazine's success—he was expected to attend parties. Of course, drinks were served and social drinking was expected. Edgar was too excited by the sudden attention he was receiving to know quite how to deal with it. He took more and more to drink, which only aggravated his already excitable nature. Then his troubles began again. He arrived late for work, or not at all. He got into tremendous shouting matches with Thomas White, owner of the *Messenger*.

It all came to a head during one especially nasty quarrel. His features distorted with passion, Edgar screamed at his boss at the top of his lungs, crying that White had no notion of what good literature was. What's more, if he had the slightest bit of sense, he would let Edgar take charge of the magazine. White had given Poe a good deal of leeway in the past, forgiving him for his drinking and his temper, but this was too much. He realized he couldn't possibly continue to work with such a man, and so he fired him. In the next issue of the magazine, White printed the following notice:

> Mr. Poe's attention being called in another direction, he will decline, with the present number, the editorial duties on the **Messenger**. . . . With the best wishes to the Magazine, and to its few foes as well as many friends, he is now desirous of bidding all parties a peaceable farewell.

Over the next three years the odd little family moved from Richmond to New York, and then to Philadelphia, as Edgar went through a series of editor's jobs. Each job ended in disaster. His problem was not only his drinking, but also his arrogance. He insisted to the magazines' owners that he knew best how a magazine should be run and what it should have in it.

It was Poe's dream to start a magazine of his own. Most magazines of the day were run by groups of literary men who published their own works and who all seemed to have the same opinions. Edgar hated these close-knit groups. In 1841, he sent out a majestic announcement that he would soon publish his own magazine, to be called the *Penn Magazine*. He wrote: "It shall be the first and chief purpose of the Magazine now proposed to become known as one where may be found at all times, and upon all subjects, an honest and a fearless opinion."

As usual, money was lacking. The *Penn Magazine* never came about and Edgar, once again, began looking for work. Meanwhile, worries about money and his heavy drinking were taking their toll. Edgar looked haggard and worn. To add to his troubles, his darling Virginia, now a lovely, frail young woman of 19, began to show signs of tuberculosis. Edgar refused to acknowledge the symptoms at first, believing that she had simply caught a chill and would soon recover. But slowly and steadily, Virginia's cheeks began to lose their childlike rosiness and an ominous cough set into her lungs.

One snowy evening in January, Poe was feeling somewhat cheerful about his life. The family had dinner guests that night, and Virginia was to play her harp and sing for them. Her adoring husband watched, so proud that his guests could see him as a normal man with a home, a wife, and a fire blazing in the

hearth. Virginia went to the harp and began to pluck the strings. A tune of enchanting beauty wafted through the room. She took a deep breath to sing.

Instead of song, a deep, wracking cough came out. Virginia coughed into her handkerchief for several seconds. When she stopped, the room was silent. Everyone stared in horror at the handkerchief. It was covered with blood. Her frightened eyes filled with tears, Virginia looked up at Edgar, her protector. The coughing of blood was the terrible, unmistakable sign of tuberculosis, what Poe called in his stories, "the Red Death."

THE TELL-TALE HEART

"I have thus rambled and dreamed away whole months,
and awake, at last, to a sort of mania for composition."

There was no mistaking the truth of Virginia's condition. Edgar's wife, his child-bride, his object of worship, was destined to die. He could not escape death. It had robbed him of his natural mother, who would have raised him with love. It had robbed him of his second mother, who would have loved and cared for him had it not been for her cruel husband. And now it was claiming his lovely wife.

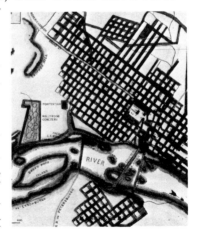

Edgar could not face this reality, and turned even more to drink. He would sit for hours with Virginia, assuring her that somehow her condition would improve. She would stare at him with her wide, bright eyes, trusting him as a child trusts a parent. But Edgar knew it was only his desperate wishes that he was telling her. In rage and pain he would fly out of the house, screaming up and down the streets, shouting his hatred for heaven and earth. He began taking opium to calm his nerves. The drug also heightened his senses and filled his mind with strange, feverish visions of terror.

Whenever he had been gone too long, Mrs. Clemm would go in search of him. Usually she found him in some cheap, dank barroom, slumped in a booth. The kindly aunt would wake him. With infinite patience, she would bring him back from the twisted landscape of dreams and visions he had drifted into. Then she would lead him home.

A day or two later, when he had recovered, he would set to work immediately. The frustration and fury that built up inside him were too intense to live with. Writing was a way to escape from the horrible real world just as alcohol and opium were. He wrote madly and intently, like a man possessed. He wrote about the eerie visions of his distant dreams. The result was something that had never been written before: horror stories.

The stories that came from his pen at this time were the most terrifying—and they were his best. "The Fall of the House of Usher" is a tale in which his imagination built upon one of his own terrors—that of being buried alive. The story is about a man named Roderick Usher whose sister has died. He has her coffin locked in the deep tomb-like cellar of his house. As the eerie story progresses, he and the friend who helped him gradually come to believe they hear a noise from below the house. In one hideous moment, days after the burial, they realize what they have done. Nearly insane with the horror of his act, Usher finally hisses the horrible truth: *"We have put her living in the tomb!"*

"The Tell-Tale Heart," also written at this time, is one of Poe's briefest and most intense stories. As with many of his tales, he does not tell the names of the characters or where they live. Poe wanted to present pure horror, unadorned by details of person and place. The story is told by a man who has senselessly murdered an old man whom he lived with. He repeatedly insists to the reader that he is not insane. Yet he says that while he loved this old man he still wanted to kill him. Eventually, it is the

man's own words that show the reader he is, indeed, insane. Poe himself was growing more and more afraid that he would lose his grip on reality, and "The Tell-Tale Heart" shows how clearly he understands the unstable mind of the murderer.

What drove the man to commit murder was the old man's eye. "Whenever it fell upon me, my blood ran cold," he says. He kills the old man. Then, to hide the body, he cuts it up and puts the pieces under the floorboards. The police come to the house because a neighbor heard a scream. The man convinces them that nothing is wrong, and they are about to leave. Suddenly, the man's own madness takes control of him. He imagines that he can hear the beating of the dead man's heart from under the boards. The beating grows louder and louder in his ears. Finally, he can stand it no more. "Villains!" he cries. "I admit the deed!—tear up the planks! here, here!—it is the beating of his hideous heart!" His insanity drives him to confess.

Poe's own "tell-tale heart" led him to create tales out of the terror and sadness that churned inside him. Like other writers and thinkers of the time, he believed that artists should focus on presenting feelings and emotions. Horror was what he felt and horror was what he wrote.

The "Tell-Tale Heart" was written about seventy years after the American Revolution. During the time of the revolution, people believed that science and reason could solve all the world's problems. By the time Poe was writing, many artists and writers had decided that science was not as important as feelings and emotions. This belief in the importance of feelings was what characterized the Romantic Movement. A "Romantic" writer, in this sense, does not mean these people wrote about love, but about all emotions.

Most Romantics, like the English poet William Wordsworth, chose to write about such subjects as the beauty of nature and the love of men and women.

I wandered lonely as a cloud
That floats on high o'er vales and hills,
When all at once I saw a crowd,
A host, of golden daffodils;
Beside the lake, beneath the trees,
Fluttering and dancing in the breeze.

Lord Byron

Poe's favorite English author, Lord Byron, was a bit different. He was a moody poet. Rather than writing of daffodils and clouds, Byron often wrote about death:

> *Death stands above me, whispering low*
> *I know not what into my ear:*
> *Of his strange language all I know*
> *Is, there is not a word I fear.*

Perhaps Byron's most famous line is: "She walks in beauty, like the night." The woman he described, so beautiful and mysterious probably appealed to Poe, who was also fascinated with strange, beautiful women.

In some ways, Poe was not a typical Romantic writer. Like others, he wrote of strong feelings. But his works were always dark with sadness, which he could never escape, or with madness, which he so dreaded.

Edgar Allan Poe did not write only tales of horror. He also wrote the first detective story. All fictional detectives, from Sherlock Holmes to today's television cops and spies, owe their existence to Poe.

Poe's detective stories came about because of his love for logic. He had unusually keen logical abilities and loved to create and solve puzzles. Logic was a way to demonstrate his genius to all the world. Once, Poe read the first chapter of Charles Dickens' new book, *Barnaby Rudge*, in a magazine. He startled the readers by writing an article in which he told the whole plot of the story—before it had even been finished! Everyone had to wait until the whole book had been printed to see if Poe was right, but one man, Charles Dickens, knew that he was. When Dickens read Poe's article, he was so bewildered that the man had been able to guess the story that he said Poe must be "a devil." Of course, it was not devilry but careful logical analysis of the first chapter that gave Poe the rest of the story.

The surprise villain of "The Murders in the Rue Morgue"

Poe's love of logic also led him to the study of cryptography, or writing in secret codes. While writing for various magazines he occasionally challenged readers to send in messages written in code, and then amazed them by publishing his decoding of the messages in the magazine's next issue. He believed cryptography could be useful for military and government secrets, and in fact it did become an important tool in later wars.

His story "The Gold-Bug" is not exactly a detective story, because there is no crime, but it does rely on logic. The characters in the story discover a paper with a coded message. If they can decipher it, the message will lead them to buried pirate treasure. The treasure is buried on Sullivan's Island, where Poe was stationed as a soldier. The story contains the secret message, and Poe shows how the secret code is deciphered.

It is Poe's tale "The Murders in the Rue Morgue" that is considered the world's first detective story. The story is set in Paris. A hideous murder has taken place but, it seems, it is impossible for any person to have committed it. Poe introduces the world's first fictional detective, C. Auguste Dupin, who puts the pieces of the puzzle together and solves the case. Poe realized that having a clever detective as the hero makes a story fun. The reader can follow the detective's reasoning and try to figure out how the crime was committed. After "The Murders in the Rue Morgue," Poe wrote two more Dupin stories.

Poe's fascination with logic seemed to grow with his dread of insanity. As Virginia slipped more and more into the clutches of tuberculosis, Poe's mind slipped farther from reality. He clung to logic and logical puzzles as a way to hold onto the ordinary, logical world. But all the while his grip was slipping.

THE RED DEATH

*"My life has been a whim—impulse—passion—
a longing for solitude—a scorn of all things present,
in an earnest desire for the future."*

n April 13, 1844, *The Sun*, a New York newspaper, appeared on the streets with the blazing notice:

ASTOUNDING NEWS!
BY EXPRESS VIA NORFOLK!
THE ATLANTIC CROSSED IN THREE DAYS!

SIGNAL TRIUMPH OF
MR. MONCK
MASON'S
FLYING MACHINE!!!

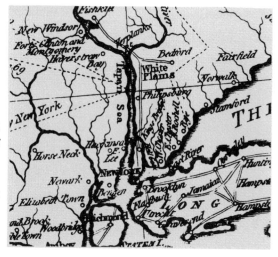

For a while, New York buzzed with the news of the astounding feat. Everyone read about the amazing balloon that made the dangerous voyage across the Atlantic Ocean—and in only three days. It seemed too wondrous to be true.

It wasn't true. The truth was that Edgar A. Poe had just moved from Philadelphia to New York in dire poverty but rich in imagination. He had dreamed up a way to make some money and, at the same time, announce his arrival in the city. "The Balloon Hoax" was the result. Poe convinced the editor of the paper to publish his story as if it were news, and for a while everyone was fooled.

The success of the story made Poe happy, and his good humor brought a smile to Virginia's face. She still had the dreadful "consumptive cough," and was terribly thin and pale, but she was feeling better lately. It seemed to Edgar that on some days she was almost completely healthy. The young couple had moved into a nice boarding house on Broadway. After living on the edge of starvation for so long, they were very happy to have a decent place to stay and good food to eat. "Muddy" was still in Philadelphia, and Edgar wrote her of their good fortune:

For breakfast we had excellent-flavoured coffee, hot and strong—not very clear and no great deal of cream—veal cutlets, elegant ham and eggs and nice bread and butter. I never sat down to a more plentiful or a nicer breakfast. I wish you could have seen the eggs—and the great dishes of meat. I ate the first hearty breakfast I have eaten since I left our little home. Sis is delighted, and we are both in excellent spirits. She has coughed hardly any and had no night sweat . . . I feel in excellent spirits, and haven't drank a drop—so that I hope soon to get out of trouble.

Soon afterwards, the happy couple had enough money to afford a house a few miles outside of town. Edgar sent for Mrs. Clemm, and once again the family was together.

Poe's wife Virginia

There were now two collections of short stories by Edgar A. Poe. *Tales of the Grotesque and Arabesque* had been published four years earlier, and *The Prose Romances of Edgar A. Poe* was put out just the year before. Besides the books, there were dozens of magazine articles, essays, and poems. Still the family had a hard time making ends meet. It was customary for publishing companies to pay writers a very small amount for their work or to pay only in free copies of the book. It was necessary for Poe to try to keep a job as a magazine editor.

Not long after the move to New York, Virginia's illness again took a turn for the worse. She was often so weak she had to remain in bed all day. She had lost more weight and her coughing had grown worse. When Poe looked into her eyes, he no longer saw the lovely face of his wife. He saw a shrinking death's head and it struck him cold with terror.

It was then that Poe, sitting in his study with its heavy purple curtains, wrote his timeless poem of sadness, "The Raven." Like all poetry of the Romantic Movement, its language is rich with rhymes and repeated sounds. And like most of Poe's writing, it is eerie:

And the silken, sad, uncertain rustling
  of each purple curtain
Thrilled me—filled me with fantastic terrors
  never felt before

The poem tells about a man sitting alone in his study on a windy night. He hears a knocking sound and, opening the window, discovers a large black raven outside. This raven is no ordinary bird, for it can speak, but the only word it knows is "Nevermore." The man thinks the bird is a messenger from beyond the grave. He asks it if, someday when he dies, he will meet his dead love, Lenore. To each of his questions the bird has the same dreary, dreadful answer: "Nevermore!"

The mournful poem poured out of Poe's heart. His own wife was still in the world of the living, but already he could sense the terrible loss, and it drove him to write the poem. Somewhere deep within himself he could still feel the pain he had felt as a three-year-old boy when death took his mother from him. The feeling of the little boy and the grown man were the same: the pain of an overwhelming sadness, and the fear of being terribly alone in the world.

When Poe finished "The Raven," he took it to the New York *Evening Mirror*, where he was working as an editor. It was published in the paper on January 29, 1845. The editors were impressed with the writing and moved by the tremendous sadness in the poem. They called it "masterly" and wrote: "It will stick to the memory of everybody who reads it."

The paper's readers responded so enthusiastically that the editors decided to print it again a week later. Soon, others heard about the amazingly sad and beautiful poem, and people everywhere were talking about it. At last, they told one another, a great American poem had been written—something that

Americans could be proud of. It would stand next to the works of Wordsworth, Shelley, and other great British writers.

Over the next few weeks, newspapers and journals around the country printed "The Raven" and millions of people read it. Within a month, it had become the most popular poem ever written by an American.

Instantly, Edgar A. Poe became a star. People wanted his autograph. Newspapers wanted to interview him. Some talked of doing away with the bald eagle and making the raven the national bird. One of Poe's nineteenth century biographers wrote, "No great poem ever established itself so immediately, so widely, and so imperishably in men's minds."

Poe was suddenly flooded with invitations to give lectures. When he spoke, hundreds of people gathered to hear him. One night at the theater, an actor spotted him in the audience. The actor nodded to Edgar and finished his lines with the words, "Nevermore! Nevermore!" All heads turned, and a thrilled whisper ran through the audience as they recognized the famous poet. At fancy parties, wives and daughters of wealthy businessmen whispered about the moody, dashing poet who wrote such elegant and mournful verse. They wondered what sort of dark, romantic life he led. His name

was on everyone's lips. "Poe!" they whispered at cocktail parties. "Poe! Poe! Poe!"

Edgar himself was sick with confusion. He basked in the attention, attended the parties, signed the autographs, but all this fame did not pay his bills. At that time there was no copyright protection for an author. A magazine or newspaper could publish a work without paying the author. "The Raven" appeared in journals all across America, as well as in England and France. It was read by millions of people, yet Poe never received a dime from it. He was still as poor as ever, and Mrs. Clemm had to scrounge through the markets looking for thin, cheap cuts of meat for the family's dinner.

What's more, Virginia's condition was steadily worsening. Poe may have become enormously popular, but fame wouldn't heal his wife's diseased lungs.

Poe was not strong enough to deal with his wondrous popularity and the approaching death of his wife. He began drinking heavily. Soon he did not show up at halls where he had promised to lecture. Friends would see him on the street, reeling from side to side, crying to the sky that the world was against him. Now that the world was at last acknowledging him as a great writer, Poe complained that he was being ignored. Slowly but steadily, he was losing his reason.

These days he was working for the *Broadway Journal*. The magazine was having serious financial problems, and its owners wanted to abandon it. Poe boldly decided to buy the *Journal* from them. In his confused state of mind, he didn't consider that he had no money or experience in managing a magazine. The only thing in his mind was his old dream of having a magazine of his own.

Poe managed to get loans to buy the *Journal* in October of 1845, but the venture was a complete disaster. He could not raise the funds to pay off the loans, and the magazine continued to lose money. In January of 1846, ten weeks after Poe took over as publisher, the *Broadway Journal* printed its last issue.

The *Journal* had stacked up enormous debts which Poe couldn't possibly pay off. His drinking problem grew worse. He would fall into fits of delirium in which he imagined all sorts of horrible creatures were attacking him. A collection of his poetry, *The Raven and Other Poems*, had been published while Poe was in charge of the *Journal*. Now he was too sick and confused to do any new writing.

When winter came, Virginia's condition became critical. She no longer got out of bed. Unable to keep warm and coughing continually, she grew weaker every day. A friend who came to visit her later wrote:

> *The weather was cold, and the sick lady had the dreadful chills that accompany the hectic fever of consumption. She lay in the straw bed, wrapped in her husband's greatcoat, with a large tortoiseshell cat on her bosom. The wonderful cat seemed conscious of her great usefulness. The coat and the cat were the sufferer's only means of warmth, except as her husband held her hands, and her mother her feet.*

The little family passed a cold, hungry Christmas that year. Instead of holiday cheer, a gloom of approaching death hung over the tiny cottage. Virginia stayed alert through the month of January, but grew weaker and weaker.

Now the images of death and the tomb that had haunted the corners of Poe's mind crowded into the forefront. Ghouls, fiends, and phantasms of every description seemed to be clamoring at him, all of them screaming one word: "Death! Death! Death!"

When Virginia first coughed up blood, Poe realized she was suffering from tuberculosis. Since then, the image of the disease, in the form of a living corpse, had haunted him. With this fearful picture in mind, he wrote one of his most terrifying stories. Another writer, faced with the death of his wife, might have written a sad tale of a beautiful dying woman. But to Poe this wasn't just a woman dying, it was his whole world. In the story, "The Masque of the Red Death," a plague of tuberculosis sweeps through a whole kingdom and destroys it. The prince of the kingdom and all of his friends lock themselves in their palace and decide to amuse themselves by having one great party until the disease is gone. But the terrifying figure of the Red Death gets in the palace, nevertheless, and everyone inside dies.

On the morning of January 31, Poe entered his wife's room and found his Virginia, his child-bride, his link with sanity, dead. To Poe, the world died with her, just as, in his story, a whole kingdom dies in agony:

> *And now was acknowledged the presence of the Red Death. He had come like a thief in the night. And one by one dropped the revellers in the blood-bedewed halls of their revel, and died each in the despairing posture of his fall. And the life of the ebony clock went out with that of the last of the gay. And the flames of the tripods expired. And Darkness and Decay and the Red Death held illimitable dominion over all.*

THE BELLS

"I was lost in reveries of death . . ."

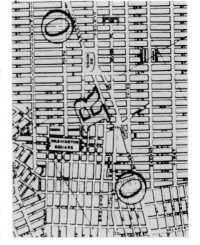

During the winter of 1847, people passing a certain New York cemetery often saw the thin figure of a man through the fence. Dressed in black and shivering with cold, the man was on his knees in front of a tomb. Anyone who ventured closer would have heard moaning nonsense coming from him. If the man had turned around, one would have seen a pale face streaked with tears, and dark eyes as cold and glassy as beads.

The man was Edgar Poe. Following Virginia's death, he spent whole days before her tomb, weeping, moaning, and begging her to come back to him. That she could never do, but soon he would go to her.

Poe's mind and body were by now so wracked by alcohol that just a few sips of a drink would send him reeling madly. Once again he turned to opium to escape from his agony.

In his weak and disordered state, it was impossible for him to work or write. The devoted Mrs. Clemm stayed with him. She kept food on the table by alerting Poe's friends and publishers of his condition and asking for their help. People contributed money, Mrs. Clemm nursed Edgar, and for a time he managed to struggle back into the real world.

A society woman named Mrs. Shaw had befriended Poe earlier. She wanted to help him to begin writing again. One evening she brought him to her house, fed him a good meal, then sat a pen and paper in front of him. She asked him to write a poem. Poe, his head aching and his vision blurred, said he could not. The bells from the nearby church were ringing, and the clanging sound echoed inside his head. "I dislike the noise of bells tonight," he said. "I cannot write. I have no subject. I am exhausted." With that, his head slumped on the table.

Mrs. Shaw took the paper herself and wrote, "The bells, the little, silver bells." She handed it back to Poe. He raised his head, looked at it, and frowned. Very poor poetry! Mrs. Shaw took the paper back and wrote, "The heavy iron bells." Again Poe frowned. This time, though, he set the paper down and, without a moment's thought, started writing.

The resulting poem, "The Bells," has very simple subject, the ringing of bells. But it is about much more. Throughout his life, Poe's mind was constantly jammed with thoughts that rang in it like bells. Sometimes the thoughts rang happily, other times they were shocking. More often, it seemed, they were frightening or sad. Poe's bells, too, rang for different reasons. So near to the end of his life of pain, sadness, and occasional happiness, Poe wrote a poem that rings with every kind of emotion. It tinkles with the happiness of a wedding:

Hear the mellow wedding bells
Golden bells!
What a world of happiness their harmony foretells!. . .
To the swinging and the ringing
Of the bells, bells, bells—
Of the bells, bells, bells, bells,
Bells, bells, bells—
To the rhyming and the chiming of the bells!

The poem clangs with the fright of alarm bells:

In the startled ear of night
How they scream out their affright!. . .
How they clang, and clash, and roar!
What a horror they outpour
On the bosom of the palpitating air!

More than anything else, Poe felt a numbing sadness in the music of bells, like the sadness when someone dies:

How we shiver with affright
At the melancholy menace of their tone!
For every sound that floats
From the rust within their throats
Is a groan.

"The Bells" was a ringing, emotion-filled poem. But its energy was not enough to lift Poe back into productive life. He continued to struggle against his dependence on drink and opium.

Poe's cottage in the Bronx as it is today

When he was sober, he swore that he would become a new man. He looked around himself for something that might help him to do so. He traveled to Richmond, his boyhood home, once again to try to start a magazine of his own.

He was unable to raise money for the magazine, but while he was in Richmond he called at the home of a Mrs. Shelton. Mrs. Shelton's maiden name had been Elmira Royster. She was none other than Poe's childhood sweetheart, the girl who had promised to marry him before he went to college. She was now a widow. Poe knew this and was hoping that she might marry him and lead him back to a sane, sober life. After the two had met several times, Poe reminded Elmira that once, long ago, they had planned to marry. He asked if she would marry him now. To his delight, she accepted. In a fever of excitement, Poe set off on September 27, 1849, for New York to bring Mrs. Clemm to Richmond for the wedding. He never arrived.

On October 3, Poe was found in a barroom in Baltimore. He was completely unconscious and had apparently been drinking for days. He was sitting propped up in a booth so that he seemed to be awake. Strangely, he was wearing someone else's clothes.

Poe was rushed to a hospital. He lived for four days, but never became completely conscious. Occasionally his eyes would flutter open and he would mumble frightened words. Sometimes he cried out that ghosts were circling his bed. At other times he would call out the name Reynolds.

In the early morning hours of October 7, he died. To this day, no one knows what happened to him on his trip from Richmond to New York. No one knows who the mysterious Reynolds might have been. Edgar Poe's death, like his life, was as dark, wondrous, and troubling as the stories and poems he left behind.

Death was the one thing Edgar Poe most feared. It haunted him all his life. It filled his mind with terrible images of the unknown.

Poe was not alone. We all have such fears. But Poe sublimated his fears into powerful writing. Perhaps this is why he has become one of the most widely read of all American authors. His works have been translated into dozens of languages. In France, Poe is considered the father of modern literature.

In the end, death, which haunted Poe, took him too. But the writer has had the last laugh. There is no more fear or terror for him. But it is we, the living, who are still haunted by Edgar Allan Poe.

A Selected Reading List

Recent Collections of the Work of Edgar Allan Poe

The Best of Poe, edited by Naunerle Farr, Pendulum Press, 1977

Complete Tales and Poems, Random House, 1975

Eight Tales of Terror, Scholastic, 1961

The Fall of the House of Usher and Other Tales, New American Library

The Narrative of Arthur Gordon Pym of Nantucket, Penguin, 1975

Poems of Edgar Allan Poe, edited by Dwight Macdonald, Crowell Jr. Books, 1965

The Portable Poe, edited by Philip Van Doren Stern, Penguin, 1986

The Science Fiction of Edgar Allan Poe, Penguin, 1976

Selected Stories and Poems, Airmont Publishers

Six Tales of Mystery and Imagination, Exeter, 1986

Ten Great Mysteries, Scholastic, 1968

Books About Edgar Allan Poe

Edgar Allan Poe: Genius in Torment, by William Jay Jacobs, McGraw–Hill, 1975

Edgar Allan Poe: Visitor from the Night of Time, by Philip Van Doren Stern, Crowell, 1973

Young Edgar Allan Poe, by Laura Benét; Dodd, Mead; 1941

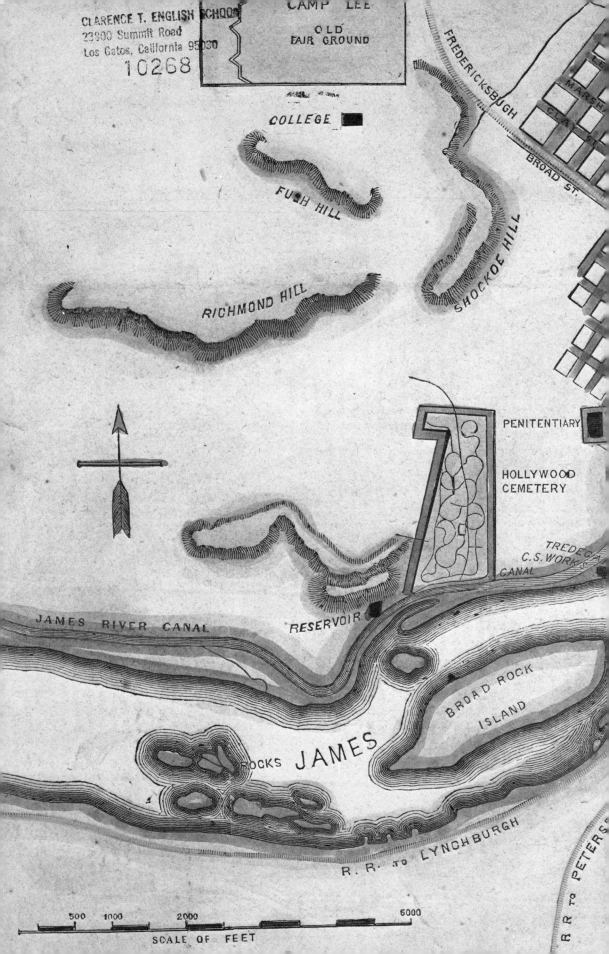